D0168800

fine

does

boy

good

every

fine
does
boy
good
every

poetry and prose

calvin arsenia

Andrews McMeel
PUBLISHING®

Special thanks to:
Justin Randall
Peregrine Honig
Brandon Jensen
Kasey Hammeke
Ashlee Fairchild Jones

And to all my friends and loved ones
who have held me gently from kiln to kiln.

This book is dedicated to
those who have been held captive
by individuals or institutions
that claim to offer freedom.

You are seen. You are heard. You are known. You are trusted.

Your story matters.

Please tell us everything.

Virgin

Family Portrait

A white picket fence in a town called Merriam
Where petunias hang heavy above our heads
Cicadas serenade us with summery vespers
Roses lounge around the yard dressed in red.

Father fires the cherry grill on Sundays
My cultured children are his delight
Kinky curls bounce off their gilded foreheads
Kicking soccer balls left and right

Mother makes her famous potato salad
Like she's done ever since I was a child.
Sparkling water tickles her freckled little nose
She sneezes, then she compliments the Italian tile

Fluffy pumpkin pancakes and hot coffee pouring
Our little family is a well-oiled machine.
My wife and kids are luminous every single morning
The ancestors would be proud of me

And to think
I gave up this dream
To put this dick
In your ass

Cul-de-Sac

When you say

"good neighborhood,"

what

exactly

do you mean?

Rituals

Every morning I watched my parents
kiss each other three times
before they would leave
and go to work.

On weekdays,
my dad left first,
and my mom would see us off to school,
but on Sundays,
my mom would pack her three children
into the family van,
kiss my father,
and we
would leave
first.

The ritual they shared
was not bound to feelings or emotion.
It was a daily reminder
of their promise and devotion.

Azaleas

She tore open the efficient curtains and
let sunlight splash through summer-soaked maples,
bounce off the very ivory pavement,
over the jittery magenta azaleas,
and into my and my brother's room.

Orange juice on ice.

My eyes clinched and clawed to
bury themselves into my brain for
protection to no avail.

What kind of cruelty is this?

I stretched to make room for my growing bones and
drank down a big yawn to make room for a big breakfast.

"Rise and shine," she exclaimed joyfully
wearing yellow rubber gloves and
carrying a pine-scent-soaked sponge.

Biscuits beckoned from the kitchen.
Gospel music wafted through the bedroom door.

"Get up and come eat. This is the day the Lord has made.
Let us rejoice and be glad in it!" she sang insistently.

My older brother's feet slumped down from the top bunk.
He plopped to the ground and followed the sound
of singing and scratched his spine with his thumb some
kind of way.

"Let us rejoice, let us rejoice and be glad!"

G'mornin'

When my father would wake me up,
he came in quietly,
rested at the foot of the bed,
and rubbed my feet until my eyes opened.
"Mo'nin'," he said.
"G'mornin'," I said back.
"Ah-ight now. Time to get up," he'd say.
"Okayyyyyy,"
and he would leave it just like that.

Sunny-Side Up

she gently broke an
egg of air
on the crown of my knee

and sent shivers
throughout
my butterscotch body

Prenup

The day after her mom came to
bring-your-parent-to-lunch day,
my first girlfriend informed me that
she was not going to marry a brown boy.

Her bangs lay straight
across her unusually green face,
and all I could think about was
how she acquired the ability to tell the future.

Precocious

The older neighbor boy told me
I'm not allowed to use words I can't spell anymore,
so I learned how to spell
"antidisestablishmentarianism"
both forward and backward
just in case.

antidisestablishmentarianism

Quality Time

My father was my hero
My very best friend
The smartest man I knew
He could fix anything

After dinner, we watched *The Simpsons*
And prime-time cartoons
Lying on the wavy waterbed
In my parents' master bedroom

Sandwich cookies and chocolate morsels
A drawer of candy on his bedside
We shared a mutual obsession for
Peanuts, caramel, and chocolate combined

Chaste

Cut flowers are virgin sacrifices
who have never known the joy of bees

Blah Blah Blah

tone-deaf
sprinklers
gush forth
in the rain

A Portal

A single June bug tied to a white string
buzzed in a circle above my head.
Candy-coated bottles of ketchup, relish, and mustard
stood as surrogate centerpieces
under the shady cedar tree.
A tower of thin paper plates and a block of white
napkins waited quietly at the end
of the plastic folding table.

The air was thick enough to ice a cake with it.
Everyone moved slowly, wiping their brow with their
wrists or the backs of their hands.
Coolers of Corona, sodas, Coors Light, and ice
offered consolation prizes for the heat.

Can we eat now?

Children dashed about. They shivered and squealed,
chucking neon water bombs at each other in the greasy breeze.
The ground beneath the blond, balding grass
was a crimson rust. Red dust discolored my shoes and my
dad's black pickup truck.

calvin arsenia

He smiled more than usual when we came back to his
grandpa's house.
My unfamiliar family all gathered around.
He passed hand-clasp half hugs to men
who looked a little bit like him.

In the kitchen,
caramel, toffee, and crème brûlée women
removed plastic wrap from salads and slaws.
They pulled molten-hot aluminum foil pans from the oven.
"Get back, boy! Get back!"

A handful of cousins
in various shapes, sizes, and shades
affixed their eyes to the big-screen television in the
living room.
I didn't know all of their names.

Tan, mahogany, ivory, cinnamon.
A light shined brightly through the prism of my grandmother's
fruitful loins to produce the rainbow of relatives that
flew in and out of that banging screen door.

every good boy does fine

FWAP!

If I wasn't hovering in the kitchen,
then you found me fluttering around
the lone lilac bush at the far end of the yard.
I admired the bunches of blooms and
counted the swollen folds of each petal.
Each buttery indigo bowl held its own private selection
of nectar.
I grew fond of the bees that feasted on these flowers.

I prayed the perfume would hold me
with both arms,
tightly,
forever.

Family Matters

I was jealous of my father's love of my mother, his wife.
I didn't know what sex was,
I just wanted to be his favorite.

Teeth Marks

The morning I said goodbye to my father like a sissy bitch when I was six.

He left me on the step there on my back,
between the living room and kitchen.
Tried my hardest not to cry.
Tears would have only been the admission
that maybe I'm not strong now,
and maybe I won't ever be.

Mama saw me all balled up
chewing on my knees.

"Do you know why your father said that?"

"Yah," I said, sniffling.

"Tell me again, what did he say, child?"

"He said, 'Boy! Get off me!'"

"Why do you think he said that, son?"

My breath was still as stone.

"He doesn't want me to be gay, Mom."

"You're right, child."

Then she left the matter alone.

Rope Burn

Faith:
Holding on to no one.
Holding on to know One.

Salt, Not Sugar

even with a mouth full of cheesy grits
my mother always understood me

One Stoplight

The water was so murky and brown
when the fire truck came to
to fill up the inflatable kiddie pool
at my aunt's country home.

Something about well water.

- Farmville, Virginia 1999

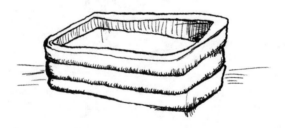

Pep Talk

You better stiffen your wrists, kid.
Someone's gonna find out what you did,
and they're gonna tell God,
and God's gonna bench you.
God's gonna get you
and decide that all of your prayers
for salvation weren't enough.
Ooooo mamamama
They're gonna teeeeeeeeell!

No, stop!
Wait!
I believe!

Self-Care

sometimes it's best to
put the brush down and
use a wide tooth comb

Are You Sure?

The small-town handyman
came to help clean up Grandma's house after she passed.
His hands knew a thing or two about concrete
and sledgehammers
and they knew very little about lotion or cuticle care.

He looked my father in the eyes
with surprise
and strangled a giggle when my father said,
"This is my son, Calvin."

He looked at me,
into my eyes,
and back to my father's,
and then back at mine,
and then to my mother's,
then to my brother's,
as if to ask why
"Calvin" had a boy name.

Puberty

how can I be a man
in a body with breasts?

Take the Solo

I was six feet tall in the sixth grade,
and I was recruited for a rec team upon first sight.

Coach gave me a ride home after my second
basketball rehearsal.

"This is the only way black men like us
get scholarships to college, you know."

I adjusted the air vent.
Pointed it directly into my face.

Squinting from the summer sun, I sat in silence,
dribbling his words,
and never touched a sportsball again.

Curfew

Ornery as I wanted to be,
I spent summer weeknights letting
the flash of light from the television screen
bounce off my smooth cheek.

While I should have been asleep,
I learned everything I needed to know about:
weight loss,
makeup,
and meal-replacement.

1(800) HELP-ME-PLEASE
1(800) SET-ME-FREE
1(800) CALL-US-ANYTIME
We are sublime
19 payments of $19.99

We are here to help you
save money by spending it.
You're becoming beautiful—
more relevant!
Your credit card,
please send it!

While my family rested,
I studied the creaky floorboards
and learned to avoid them.
Featherlight, almost flying,
my feet didn't touch the ground.

Fire Insurance for a Nine-Year-Old

"If you want to be sure that
if you died right now
that you would spend eternity with
Jesus, then repeat after me:

God"

                                              "God"

"I know I have sinned and
fall short of Your glory"

                          "I . . . think I have sinned and . . .
                                fall short of Your glory"

"And I want to make it right tonight"

                          "And I want to make it right tonight"

"Please forgive me"

                                    "Please . . . forgive me"

"I turn from my wicked ways—"

                          "I turn from my wicked ways—"

"—and accept the Lord Jesus Christ
as my personal Lord and Savior."

"—and I accept the Lord Jesus Christ
as Lord and Savior."

"Thank you, God, for your wonderful gift."

"Thank you, God for y—"

"In Jesus' holy name."
The word "holy" was almost sung.

"In Jesus' name"

"And everybody said:"

Everyone joining in audibly, including me,
"Amen"

The Mayonnaise Doesn't Fall Very Far from the Refrigerator

my mother's bookshelves
sagged
with self-help and shame

Dirty December, January, and February

There were months of my life
I did not see my naked body.
I would avoid showering until
the stench started reaching out
through the collar of my shirt and
interrupted conversations.

To avoid further ridicule,
I would shower, quickly,
long enough to fog up the mirror good and soggy
so I wouldn't have to
lay eyes on the animal
beyond the mist.

Real Talk

How I got fat:
I ate too much.

Whoops

A file I downloaded was misnamed and
rather than it being the animated children's film I was after,
it was something else.

I watched the whole thing
and deleted it and
noticed something cool and damp on my lap
coming from inside my light-wash jeans.
I got up and went to the bathroom.
Dropped my pants to check.
Did I just pee myself?

Fame Game

Dozens of celebrity Christians
graced the stage of my beloved
childhood church.
At school, I would talk about the ones
I shook hands with.

I'm sure everyone in our
congregation did the same.

And the church continued to grow.

Your Signature Here:

"Good evening, everyone, and welcome to the True
Love Waits Banquet!"

The extremist I am
made a commitment at that round table
that I would not only abstain from sex with a woman
but that I wouldn't even kiss a girl
until that holy moment,
at our wedding,
in the presence of our friends and loved ones.

By God,
I would remain clean for her.
Untainted.

Exit Clause

Failure does not exist in Fundamentalism
If something doesn't work out, it wasn't God's plan

It wasn't your fault
You were outside of the will of God

Dirt Lip

I Was Ready

The school bell rang, and the passing period
chatter lulled itself to sleep.
I always slouched a bit because nothing was
more embarrassing than,
"Teacher, I can't see the board over his head!"
Slumping down was a preventative measure.

Biology was my favorite class besides choir.
Beakers and Bunsen burners lined the classroom
on either side.
We faced the teacher's desk, and a large whiteboard
guarded the wall behind it that
spanned the entire width of the room.
Fluorescent lights hummed above our heads
as we studied the intricacies of God's creation—
how symmetry, synchronicity, and symbiotic relationships
symbolized the grip that
God had on His beautiful world.
His fingerprints were on everything.

My biology teacher was young,
recently out of college.
Vibrant and practical.
Circular light-colored glasses.
Active yet homely physique.
Comfortable clothing.

calvin arsenia

It was no secret she was a Christian.
The students of my school Bible study
actively kept accurate tabs on who our faculty allies were.
She was one of us.

Though I loved studying ribosomes and mitochondria,
I braced myself all semester long for the inevitable
Evolution unit:
The dreaded antithesis of Jesus Christ Himself.
Years of church study had
made me ready for this.
I had been given marching orders and a strategy.

As a member of a congregation of modern thinkers,
it was my honor and duty to disperse and disseminate
accurate information to my classmates and teachers,
to spread the good news of Noah's flood,
the inaccuracy of carbon dating,
and the list of he-begot-he's to conclude that the
world is in fact
only several thousands of years old,
which wouldn't be enough time for
primordial goo to become the statuesque
humans, beasts, and
flowers we have before us today.

every good boy does fine

We recited verse after verse,
filled out worksheets and study guides,
watched VHS tapes on boxy convex TVs,
and armed our minds with the information required to
defend a seven-day creation.
Actually, it was just six days.
On the seventh day, He rested.
Didn't get up.

The day our teacher introduced the Evolution unit,
I wondered whether she would honor our Great Lord
and Savior
or disgrace Him.

She surprised us all like this:
"Today, we are going to talk about evolution.
I know this is a sticky subject, but it is a part of our
required curriculum so we have to study it."

All of the students, including myself, held our breath.

"Before we begin, I would like to explain that science is
not something to believe in—
it is a system of observation and record-keeping.
Evolution is a theory,
and a theory is the practice of deduction
based on a series of observations.

No one was around when everything happened,
and there are many theories about what took place
before we started writing everything down.

Since we weren't there, all we have
is what we can see now.
It is important that we are informed of
as many theories as possible.

Please keep an open mind."

We let out a collective sigh of relief.

I spent a semester of fear and anxiety looking forward
to this day,
envisioning myself standing on that cold slate desk,
tearing Darwin apart,
and dismantling modern science cell by cell.

There was no bang.

There wasn't anything.

Girl Jeans. Dear God. Girl Jeans.

Carson.
Guy-liner Carson.
Emo-banged-hair-toss Carson.
Trumpets-from-on-high-angel-man Carson.
Jelly-bracelets-up-and-down-his-left-and-his-right-arm
Carson.

How can you be so free in your forever-changing body?
Are you going to be suspended for making obvious
sexual references on your shirt?
Will you be expelled for being openly gay?
Who brought you to school this morning?
Does your mom still love you?

My mom won't even let me wear a shirt with words on it.
"You aren't a billboard, son."

Generic Worship, Aughts

The sound was like an ocean's waves,
people from wall-to-wall singing
their own unique songs to Jesus.
I stood there taking it all in.
People singing
and praying
and shouting
in English,
Korean,
Spanish,
Mandarin, and
the tongues of angels.

What is this?

The following pages are excerpts from prayer journals
I kept as a teenager.

These writings have been largely untouched except for
necessary grammatical and formatting changes.

every good boy does fine

In December of 2005,
I attended a conference not knowing that
this would be a time of shifting for me.
The event, called *********, catapulted me
into a new understanding of how
the Uncreated God desired to know my heart &
wanted that same unquenchable love from me in
return.

My eyes were opened!
Raging passion for this bottomless
well of love & life (that I now have access to)
filled my being—
even the depths of me.
Now, I long for the deep things of God &
He of me.

Hypothesis:

This life is merely preparation for the one to come—
the resolution of the masterpiece.

Once that has come,
we start the second book.

We've spent the last 7,000 years digging in—
now let's build skyscrapers.

The life that is to come is going to be so great.
The most intense form of intimacy.
Knowing Him in His completeness.
Partnership with Him.

We were made to fulfill a purpose of companionship.

This life is mere preparation for the rest of eternity.

I imagine colors in a brilliance unknown to men.
I imagine flavors that have yet to be imagined.
I imagine music that sounds like the Spirit.
I imagine fierce love that consumes.

What is it going to be like
when You walk with us again?

"Thank You"
will not begin to describe
the appropriate response to
something like what You
have done for me.

I have experienced this wound.
I see the history and
the use of this testimony.

Lord, I ask for the grace to leave this life behind me and
walk forth in freedom.

Make the wounds into
a beautiful picture
that displays the reach and
journey to where I now live.

Let our relationship
flourish tonight.

Teach me your ways so that I can know You.

I want to walk to the rhythm of Your beat.

every good boy does fine

Can I find myself in love w/ You again?
I need Your truth

Though I am dark, You say I am lovely

Praise You! GOOD JOB! Your plans in this life for me
are awesome. Would You let me in to see what else You
have in store for me?

I love that You are close. I love that I have a church that
loves Your truth.
Let me develop a lifestyle that really is with You!

I wanna be lovesick

I am DESPERATE
Thank You for being You
You're awesome!
Your grace is necessary for me!
I love You.

It amazes me & perplexes me
how I call myself a "Christ-one,"
and I hardly know Christ.

I'm convinced that this is an epidemic among a lot of
the church today.

A part of me is also convinced that you shouldn't have
to tell someone that you are a Christian.

They will know us by our love.

I make my requests known to the Father.
Jesus, my intercessor, has relayed my request despite
the fall.

"It's on me."

And the Holy Spirit works on the earth to have these
things be done.
Each expression of God is different and necessary.

Lord, Most High King, show us Your love.
There is so much more to Christianity than
simply rules and trying to enforce them.
The way we are wired demands that we love something.
Everyone has a passion.

I want NOTHING more than to be used by God!
(trinity)

every good boy does fine

At the end of the day, Jesus wins
The enemy has & will be defeated

Teach me to kill my flesh. It hinders me.
Teach me to love You better. This strengthens me.
Teach me to be weak; live desperately.

Who the Son sets free is free indeed

I am so easily taken off track
I long for the light
I live in the black

Teach me to love like You love

Hell will not prevail

All flesh is grass, fading away
Only You last, only You remain

In our secret place
I long to see Your face
To feel Your embrace
My life to waste

In our secret place
I long to hear Your voice
Be rid of all the noise
I make it my choice
To be deep, deep, deep
In You

So I return to my first love
Of this world, I've had enough
I return to my first love
After You, I run

Give me a fresh revelation of the nearness of You

I love being close to You
        Whisper tenderly into my heart and
                Wake me from the inside

You are beautiful
        Woo my heart
                Draw me away
                        Reveal to me the love
                                You have for me
Love that is violent
        Love that is true
                Life-giving fountain
                        Love that is You

True love only comes from the Father
        This, our Father of lights
                This love that demands my everything
                        My talents, my time, my rights

You cause distress to my insides
        Death has ridden those you love
                & it's not that You haven't made a way
                        You said, "call to me, just call

above"
There is something beautiful in this frustration
My heart longs for You to reign
Touch the hearts in this nation
Bring Your mercy before the
torrential rains

You've loved me when I'm broken
You love me when I'm weak
You love me though I'm silent
I've not one word to speak

The darkness will soon shatter
The earth will soon shake
Our spirits yearn and rattle

ARE YOU AWAKE?

Testify or Test If I'm Lying

On the Sunday after high school church camp,
all the campers wearing the same shirt
are invited to be on stage during the big Sunday service
to testify about their encounters with the person of
Jesus Christ Himself
in hopes that their parents will come
and these parents will bring their money
to invest in a program that over the course of one week
changed their children significantly enough
to say things like:

"God saved me from my addiction to cigarettes
when I finally surrendered myself to Him."

And

"I was going to kill myself, but
this week I got saved!
One night during worship,
Jesus encountered me in a vision, and
I felt His deep unending love for me."

And

"I know my mother has been praying for me.
I believe God answered her prayers.

The word of God says that when
we honor our father and mother
our days will be long and,
today I am here to say that
I will be seeing you in heaven, Dad!
I gave my life to Christ."

Church Scandal

No one wants to be a church scandal.
It is the worst.
Imagine being a senior pastor at a major church
somewhere in the middle of America.
Your weekend services are filmed by a full-on TV
production team.
Youthful and diverse musicians flock to rock in your
elaborate sanctuary.
You wear makeup to appear less ghostly on screen.
Your words have the power to set and shape
the culture and political views of your parishioners.
You study and learn and grow and grow the church and
teach the people what is right and moral
for a god-fearing father to allow their sons and
daughters to do.
You teach the women how to honor their hardworking
husbands.
You define what is right and what is wrong.

No one wants to be a church scandal.
It is bone-crushing.
Imagine being the most loved pastor at a church
just east of the Rockies and every human you
encounter,
friend, family, or foe, looks to you as a self-declared
moral compass.

calvin arsenia

Looks to you for direction on where to go next and
how to get there.
Looks to you for how to vote in the next election.
Looks to you for how to deal with difficult questions.
Looks to you when the world is falling apart.
Looks to you when the family is in question.
Looks to you when marriage is falling apart.
And what do you do?

You tell them what they believe is the truth:

Man shall not lie with mankind as with womankind.
It is an abomination.

And yet, you, senior pastor,
lie with mankind.
You pay mankind a visit every once in a while,
and pay for mankind's services.

Mankind watches you
in bronzer and Aqua Net
on your regional Sunday morning television broadcast
damning homosexuals,
condemning homosexuality,
and praising the sanctity of heterosexual marriage.

every good boy does fine

Mankind calls up the news to tell them that you're a liar.
That you lie to mankind
because you lie with mankind on your days off in secret,
and mankind was tired of being called an abomination.
He's tired of
the lies.

Imagine
when your church finds out
what you have done.
When your wife finds out what you have done.
What now,
oh great moral compass?
What do we do with you?

Smash you against the rocks?
Melt you down and turn you into something else—
something useful that aligns with God's ideals?
Chuck you into the valley below?

No one wants to be a church scandal.
It is the fiery teeth of hell.
Whatever shall we do with you, pastor?
WWJD?

Him + him

Will You Sign My Cast?

he broke my heart
first and worst.

Elephant

He didn't even go to church
I knew him from school

We just started to hang out
just us two,

"I can give you a massage."

Touching his arms and his shoulders, one at a time,
kneeling now on the floor by his left side,
his upper back, his nape, his serpentine spine.

I was lost in his tissues.
Soft, shallow, and fine
his sturdy bones connecting his beautiful slender frame
together.

I felt pressure
building between my legs.
My cargo shorts inflating

"There's a new Christian venue downtown.
Have you heard of it?"

A Recipe for Reciprocation

His mother's house was scummy with the stale aroma
of fast food.
The living room was "well-loved."
The beige carpeting was a scrapbook of tipped sodas,
juice, movie nights, and
adolescent buttery popcorn paws.
The couch matched the floor.

We were getting ready to leave to get food
when his mother came in with groceries.

"I'm going to take a shower," he said, leaving the room.
He hated being in a room with his mother.
Even the thought of her turned him to stone.

His mother radiated when she entered the room,
always wearing a smile that cost her something.

Everyone was home that afternoon. Except stepdad.
I was in a long overcoat that I had gleefully procured
from a thrift store.
Why take such a garment off, even in summertime,
when I look so good in it, and
it was oh so very, very cheap?
My thriftiness ought to be praised.

I continued making small talk with his mother,
overcompensating
for the fact that her son and I had been intimate multiple times
though we never kissed.

Stiffen your wrists, kid, or else she'll suspect something.
Lower your voice.
Darken your tone.
Be overly kind to her
because when she finds out,
if she finds out,
she will love this memory of us.
She will mention this during her toast at the wedding.
Her blazing grin will overcome the audience.
She will be the one to make this OK.

He peeked his head around the corner at me
flashing a bit of his golden shoulder.
The conversation with his mother had naturally puttered,
and he made a gesture for me to come down the hall.

I said not a word and I followed.
I would have followed him into the center of the sun.

When he stayed at his mom's house, he slept in the basement.
It was odd for us to be upstairs at all.
I had never been down this dark hallway before.

every good boy does fine

Those jeans.
That stance.
That swagger.
Those hands.

The next thing I know
he's in the bathroom.
No—we're in the bathroom.
He's in the shower,
naked.
Light splashes through a narrow window above his
head.
Streaks appear on the steamy mirror.
The door is shut behind me.

I am locked in, and I cannot leave.
What is the narrative here?
Why am I in here with you when they are all around?
You are ruining our chances of ambiguity!

Trampling footsteps zoomed past the door.
Squealing, laughing, whining, bickering.
Kids just being kids.
Oh, God!

What do you want to happen right now?
Tell me anything, and I will do it!
Say something. I'm yours.
Give me instructions.

calvin arsenia

I wish I could say what happened next was so hot,
that I stripped down, and
we finally kissed and made love like I had always wanted to,
or that he grabbed me by the collar and
we were drenched in the downpour of his steamy shower.
I wish I could tell you that he finally confessed his undying
love for me,
that the women he would bring around sometimes weren't
doing it for him.
He wanted to take us seriously. Publicly.

No.
This wasn't that.

He pressed a hand against the wall,
tipped his head,
and let the water fall down his long
body.

He left a little sliver of an opening
just enough for me to see him
naked.
A little gift for me.
Maybe for making his mother feel seen when he could not.
Maybe for being kind to his siblings.
Maybe for the months he slept next to my side saying
nothing.
In either case, whatever his reasoning,
I received every drop he was willing to pass my way.

every good boy does fine

He dried off in front of me.
My face was moist.
I pretended to look away so as to play along
and asked him what his plans were for that weekend.

He had to work.
He always had to work.

We left together, and I drove us to get sandwiches.
Me, a spicy Italian sub with
all the vegetables and extra dressing.
Him, no mayo, no mustard.
Just turkey and Swiss.

Bella Vista

ignorance is bliss
knowledge is euphoria

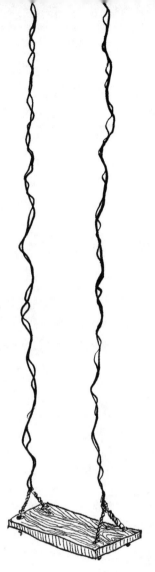

Plumbing

we don't care what swings between
your legs or doesn't swing

just be a good person
and give respect

every good boy does fine

29" x 32"

there was a time in my life
when I thought
all gays wore skinny jeans

An Audience of One

My first time living away from home
was my first time being away from you.
I followed a call from God and
became a missionary overseas.

In my third month away,
you video called me in the middle of your night
from your mother's couch.
It was such a relief to hear
the sound of your tongue touch your teeth.

We exchanged words
long enough to realize
words were not what either of us
really wanted.

As quietly as I could,
in coded language,
I asked if you would do me a solid
and show me
yourself.

You did
and you were solid
and then I knew
your body loved me, too.

every good boy does fine

We lost connection.
The screen went black.

When I called you back,
over and over,
you didn't answer.

There must have been a bad connection.

Then a message appeared.
With words that have never lost their sting:

"I see you as a brother in Christ,
not as a lover."

Things you can say to yourself when you feel like
giving up:

OK sure.

Your Tongue Is a Wand

if you don't like the magic,
cast a different spell

The Tables Have Turned

you raise your hands to Jesus
while I'm sitting in a room
writing songs about you

Flatline

people are people.
no one is special.
everyone is extraordinary.
it is the exact same thing.

Replacement

my guitar shares the bed with me
she keeps me company
when you're not around

Luxe

I got so many options
the week I do laundry
to wear whatever I want

Simply Put

I wanna be
naked
with you

Abs

there was a time in my life
when I thought
all gays were naturally fit

Bar Food

I've reserved these nuts for you,
come and get them while they are hot!

First Steps

if I'm honest with myself,
I haven't been honest with myself

Pregame

the most exciting thing I'll do today
is secure poison for tonight

every good boy does fine

Split Down the Middle

drunk glitter fuckboy
you know you have church in the morning

you better run home, boy
before that shot you took
takes you down

Blur

the "open" sign
is a string of light
if you spin around fast enough

every good boy does fine

Happy New Year

picking out vomit sediments
semen-ted into my wild pubic hair

a sentiment

Fur Baby

Every time I wake up to a brand-new guy,
I turn to either my left or my right
and ask myself,
"Could I cherish this face for the rest of my life?"

My face, swollen and puffy,
guck in my eyes.
Sleeping Prince Charming,
purring nearby.

I know it's stupid—
he's a stranger at best,
but there's something beautiful about
a beast at rest.

Bad Math

you equate pain for passion
like some other men do

Under-Promise, Over-Deliver

his dating profile was pretty sparse and since
I'm mostly attracted to emotionally unavailable men,
I knew it was true love

Snack Time

He's got options,
so many options,
he can have any size or color he wants—
that's the perk of being beautiful.

Twenty-first century man,
I really wanna see you again.

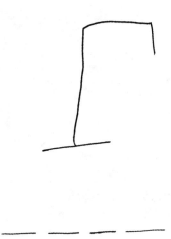

commitment is a
four-letter
word to him

Gateway

Inject me with your dopamine,
but man, I hope your shit is clean

Yet

It's been one month since you've said anything sincere to me.
Two weeks since my birthday.

"We can't be
lovers
yet."

You told me what I wanted to hear,
and I gave myself freely to you.
That if I bore the weight of us,
our mutual love could blossom and bloom
and people would come from miles away
just to bask in its splendid perfume.

I held on until the fragrance grew weary.

I had played all the cards I had to deal,
presented all the spectacles I had to show,
recited all the lines I had remembered,
showed up and put out,
with a butter-stained brown paper bag full of
homemade tiny apple pies
stacked one on top of the other.

You ate them all yourself.

every good boy does fine

Perhaps we both did the best we could
with the resources we had.

There is much less of me now that I have given
all of me
to you.

Your eyes were sapphires—
seas my heart voyaged in secret.
Seeking islands of shelter
knowing full well there were none in sight.
Nothing to cling to but

yet.

Physics

you don't mean to hurt those you love
you just do

A Riddle

I have your heart but
I don't have you

Those First Three Nights Were Pretty Wild

Beard
Queer
Beer
Cheer
Tear
Clear
Glitter
Bedsheets
Cups of tea
Edinburgh
Two-story buses
Grey
Gold
Blurry
Slurring
Kiss
Hold
On top
Squeeze
MUAH!
Snack
Breakfast
Bust
Spoiled
Milk
Mold

every good boy does fine

Mildew
Ginger
Green
Blue
Bewilder
Shortbread

Sit-Down Dinner

sink your teeth into my ripe flesh.

salty,
sticky,
sweet,

don't put me in a pan
or a storage container.
enjoy me now.
don't save me for later.

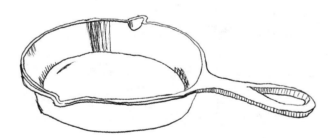

Bite-Sized

melt in my mouth
not in my hand

You are my cigarette.

You are my cigarette.
After a long hard day, I crave you.
When my stomach is full, and I hear the evensong,
I long to hold you in my fingers.
I need to put you on my lips,
I have to breathe you in
deeply.

Slowly in, quickly out.
Always, always deep.

Too long without you gives me headaches and heartburn.
Too long without you makes my edges sharp,
slicing through casual conversations,
relinquishing my carefree, cashmere Calvin-ness.

When I breathe you in, and all is quiet.
All is well.

I don't want to quit you.

You are my cigarette,
and our encounters require your nonchalant burning.
You don't preserve yourself for anyone.
Yes, you are in my fingers, my lips, and my lungs,
but your flaming skin turns to ashes.

every good boy does fine

I recall the initial hazing:
our bones alight with lusty inhalations,
your musk I bathed in. Eagerly wheezing.
Blowing smoke down my chimney.
We disabled the alarms.

Without meaning harm,
you left marks
from the times when you got too close.

From now on, all of my lovers will know.
For my garments are smudged with a tinge
of your legendary stink.
My fingers yellowed.
My lips crimped.
My lungs black and gummy.

You are my cigarette, and
I'll quit when I'm good and ready.

Physics P.2

I broke my heart on you.
It's just something I do.

I Thought I Was Doing the Right Thing

four shots of whiskey
two for me and
two for you

I'm delivering bad news and
you're not going to take this well

Worn Out

this must be
what my liver feels like

Boy, Was I Wrong

there was a time in my life
when I thought
all gays were accepting and kind

A Notion

he was an almond croissant,
layered and sweet,
almost made a mess in my lap.

I declined his invitation to
to breakfast at the Swiss patisserie
because a church piano,
however miraculous,
just can't play itself.

Angry

Angry you were beautiful.
Angry that you'd kiss me
in the soft azure light of a pearline moon,
on the roof of your building,
in the shadow of the bell tower.
With stars in your eyes,
you spun and twirled,
kicks and all,
and sang Joni's "A Case of You"
directly into my mouth—
right down my throat.

I tasted and listened
with my fullest attention.

Fuck.

I'm angry at myself
for getting ensnared in you.
I didn't heed the warnings I was given countless times,
"This could happen to you. Be careful.
Every rose has its thorns."
But
I know roses.
I know their thorns.
The aroma is worth the risk.

calvin arsenia

Angry you kissed me.
Angry how much I liked it.
Angry I felt like you were out of my league.
Angry you called me.
Angry you thought I'd be down for a no-strings kinda thing
Don't you know I'm a string fiend?
Angry we shared trauma—
cross-shaped scars.

Angry you smelled so good
especially in that spot right below your belly button.
Was that a natural scent?

Angry I melted when I was around you.
Angry I misplaced my mind
between the cushions of your vintage mustard couch
next to the stained-glass window.
Angry that my friends had to catch my ugly tears—
their shoulders were puddles in the wake of you.

Angry I was addicted.
Angry you were my dealer.
Angry you were the only thing I wanted that summer,
and fall,
and winter.

every good boy does fine

Angry you kissed me in the aisle at your work
in front of an audience of clearance items
dangling on hooks.

You were the first person to kiss me in daylight.
That was your move.

Angry I made a shrine to that moment in my mind.
Angry I spent time worshipping at that shrine.

Angry I didn't tell you I had a runny nose that night.
I thought you would find me less angelic,
so I took twice the dose recommended
(orangey, spicy, thick)
and came to your roach-infested place anyway.
Angry I could have gotten you sick.

I'm angry that it took a fistful of years
and a wardrobe of lovers
to realize that
I'm angry that I wasn't comfortable being naked around you
or myself.

Angry I got crabs and
I didn't tell you.

Is that why I didn't hear from you?
Did you give me your pets?
Or did I get them from that model traveling through town?
Angry we couldn't talk about it.

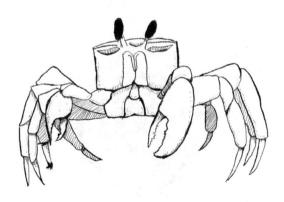

Where Are You Now?

can you see me
wiping last night's makeup
off my face?
I thought this was Your ministry.
I thought You were into this sorta thing.

Strength

he asked if
we can
be friends

for the first time
I was able to
say

no

_ _ _ _ **P.2**

when you're thinking of me
I'm thinking of running away

Artist vs. Artisan

you are not my muse
you are just the boy
I dumped my load into
sorry for the misunderstanding

Presence

when you returned to me,
a bit of your innocence was missing.
where did you leave it, babe?

Nature

there was a time in my life
when I thought
all gays came from dysfunctional families

Nurture

there was a time in my life
when I thought
all gays created dysfunctional families

calvin arsenia

Hyde Park, Kansas City, MO

my little corner of the universe
is a drafty old addition in a
mid-century home.

I never started a family,
and there is no punchline.

Could I Have a Cannoli, Please? The One on the Left

I suppose one could potentially discover the love of
their life
in the hallway of a folk festival in Kansas City.
I mean—
it wouldn't be the weirdest thing I had ever heard of.

I gauged him by my very odd yet practical standard of
"Could I spend years waking up next to this face?"

His face was nice and pleasant.
Lots of boyish smiles,
sparkly eyes,
and a persistent five o'clock shadow.

The nicks and cuts told me he was insecure about his
overall hairiness,
but that was something I quite liked about him.

We rolled around a hidden hallway above the hotel
mezzanine,
then sent letters and postcards that were sweet and
full of sentiment,
and when I arrived in Boston
to follow this fiddle player around the city,
I wasn't interested in seeing any of the traditional relics.

calvin arsenia

I wasn't too put off by the fact that he had a deep
hatred for melted cheese
and yet still insisted we eat Italian food.
I didn't care that his bed was literally in a closet
'cause he smelled nice.

But when he turned out the light,
and turned over
and said goodnight,
there was no sweetness.
And trust me,
body autonomy is everything.
I didn't want him to be uncomfortable,
but I did not get on a plane to Boston for this.

Evicted

yeah
I'm an artist
but don't call me starving
I eat every day and
home is where the heart is

Nuance

there was a time in my life
when I thought
all gays loved drag

Z z z Z Z Z z z

Night Cap

we only just met
as glitter bugs in your doorway
where we had our first kiss
and I'm already snoring

Arthur's Seat

We took a walk
on a moonlit night
into a park
in the middle of the city.

There was a chill in the air,
but my body was hot.
I took my shirt off
which I never do
stone-cold sober.
We kissed and sang
into each other's mouths
in harmony.

Emotional Side-Hugs

we can keep it surface
if you want.
this isn't the first time
I've had to pretend to be shallow.

Mislabeled

when you call me *independent*,
I can't think of a single time
when I'd rather be alone

What is "Gay Church"?

there was a time in my life
when I thought
all gays hated Jesus

Brownnoser

Perfectly Simple

When I wake up with him,
I have to stop myself from kissing him awake since
he works the night shift.
I try to let him sleep a bit more
until I can't resist the sweetness,
and I kiss him anyway.

We met on a hookup app,
and within weeks,
it looked like this:

                                          I think I like you

I like you, too <3

                                             So
                What happens if we keep liking each other?

I guess we just keep liking each other then

And this is why we are together

But there was also this:

calvin arsenia

Let's just commit to being good to each other
Whoa
That's like
So perfectly simple
I can do that
:)

And

I don't need a savior
I need a partner
Someone to walk beside me
Someone to watch my back

A Rainbow Connection

I am red
  your lips after we've been kissing

yellow
  a street sign screaming caution

orange
  marigolds in the McDonald's parking lot

green
  the soft lawn of the Nelson-Atkins Museum

blue
  your eyes as they careen over the Missouri river

violet
  with bruises. I kick myself for biting my tongue

I am yours
  gas station checkout line flowers

Ugly Cry

you're the kind of guy
I would ugly cry in front of
and this makes me wanna
ugly cry

Jigsaw

we make puzzles
puzzles of cuddles
and I can't pick one
I like more than the others

his ears pinked

How to Measure Self-Esteem

he makes me feel so good
I gotta lift my rearview mirror

A Transcription

I know that
Um
The way I use my tongue
Is very
Um
Unusual for people like us
And um
One example of that
Is I realized I kept um
Saying thank you
To you
While we were having sex a few nights back
And
And
It's because
I have made a commitment to myself
And to the people that I care about
That I won't edit myself
Because
The people who I love
Or like
Or whatever
Who are around me
I owe it to them
To know me
Anyway

every good boy does fine

Um
I said thank you multiple times to you
Because I was so grateful for what is
What felt like to me
Um
Ya
Just an undeserved favor
Like um
Like appreciation or something by you
And I was just so happy to be in that moment with you
And then you said thank you back
Maybe the next night
Maybe that night
I don't remember
And it was so hot
Because
Rather than simply being an object
That happens to be alive
Gratitude
Um
Is kind of a personification or something
Like it is admitting
The subject to whom you are speaking
Is a human
Has thoughts and feelings
Wants to be appreciated

And I just want to say that
I felt very close to you
Then
A kind of intimacy
That I'm not familiar with
But look forward to more,
I know is a potential now,
And
Um
I hope this makes your ears feel good
soft chuckle
Ya
That's all

Badges

insults I used to be offended by but
now just think of what I was joyously
participating in last night:

brownnoser
ass-kisser
cocksucker
fudge-packer

Read Receipts

a kiss that's blown
and isn't caught
is a message left
unread

Bee Honey

be honey

show me
that contentment
isn't a crime

calvin arsenia

Supply and Demand

I am always preparing
to say goodbye
I keep my distance
you think I am shy

Go on, go shopping
for my heart on a shelf
I've got a stash in the back
I keep all for myself

Relocate

I cannot live where
God throws tantrums
and speaks only through
broken prophets
to remind me
there is nothing I can do
to save myself

In the Room

I saw him
again
at a work event

it had been
seven years since
the incident

his hair's gone gray
his waistline has changed
but his hands and the way
he holds them are the same

No Thanks

if Heaven's where you're gonna be
I'm going to the other place

I know there's no room
for soft boys in your Heaven

You Get to Know Me Now

I'd rather you hate me for me than
love me for who I am not

Confectionately,

every good boy does fine

For Elijah

Confectionately,
for years
my peers
addressed me like
I was a

chocolate sandwich cookie
filled with soft vanilla cream.

I'm the whitest
black man
they ever did see.

And I let them
think that of me.

Can we take him home, please?
I want to show him to my dad!

This Isn't Complicated

my American heritage
reaches back
to the early 1700s

I am the child of both
slave and master

biologically diverse
and yet I am labeled black

(5% rule)
(by the way, that's racist)

Alice

I was 28
the first time I saw the face
of my
great
great
great grandmother
Alice—
a centenarian
who was born a slave
and died a free woman

even though
we would disagree on
the matter of Jesus,
we share a love
of red roses
and reading

Command+Z

I'm trying to undo systemic racist structures
by becoming closer to my father and my brothers
sharing my emotional experiences with them
and editing myself less when I talk to them.

We deserve to know each other.

Midas

I paint my nails gold because
life is precious
I am the luckiest
and I'm not afraid anymore

calvin arsenia

Is There a Candy Bar Fundraising Campaign for Us?

I am realizing
I am an endangered species.

Still

I'm tired,
but I'm not giving up yet.
Still black.
Still gay.
Still proud,
but mostly just

      still.

Fuck February.

Black history
is American history.
May the two never part.

every good boy does fine

You will not erase me

Flip the Script

they bought us to build it
not to live in it
I see these truths to be
self-evident

Internal Conflict

they Aunt Jemima'd Dr. King
gave him his own day
a chapter in our textbooks
and named a street after him
that runs through the black part of town

Cleaver II said he was ashamed of his city
for holding on to its own history but
I am ashamed that the only black men this country honors
are the ones who they kill

A Reflection

you are the face
of a new America

← draw a
self-portrait
here

Can I Bring My Partner?

I don't want to be associated with guilt.
I don't take pleasure in pain.
I want to create something beautiful,
to eat delicious food,
to share at the potluck,
to laugh at the stories,
and to be free to share mine,
to hold the grieving,
to be held at the same time,
'cause we are all the same.

I don't want handouts
if they are peppered with guilt,
but I would love to enjoy the bounty of your harvest
if you would enjoy mine.

Be Good

you better be good
else we'll own you
again

this is what I hear
when you say
"back the blue"

Super

I wanna be
Chadwick Boseman
staring out over
Wakanda

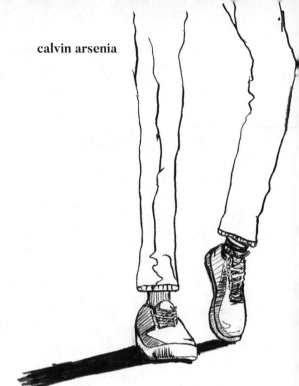

calvin arsenia

Autonomy

I am free
where I stand

Red Lines Drawn in Blood

The "Jesus' Life Matters" sign
on Ward Parkway
near the Country Club Plaza
is up-lit after nightfall.

Between the lines,
behind the blinds,
I am not welcome.

Color-splaining

Black is not the color of my skin.
It is the rubric by which you judge me,
the history you use to see me,
the music you think I know about,
the movies you think I've seen,
the foods you think I prefer,
the culture you think I represent,
my habits,
my fashion,
my accent—
please,
tell me more!
I insist—

It's Me or the Candy Bar

yeah,
please,
I'll take my receipt—
without it
my life
could not
matter

Reframing

managing happiness is
managing expectations

managing expectations is
managing happiness

Toughen Up

You say
I am weak,
bent, and soft

to justify handling me gently.

I assure you,

though you label me as weak,
I am nimble;
what you see as bent
is ergonomic,
and where you see me as soft,
I see padded.

Life is hard on all the living,
and we are born with ways to survive it.

Creases

tiny crows have been stomping
on your face
leaving footprints
'cause you're laughing so hard
all the time

Doing Fine

no one is concerned
about my
aging face
but me

An Evening in Our Winter Garden

Well I dunno, man,
I know it sounds rude,
but I'm not trying to
grow old at all, dude.

When I'm all grayed out
and my skin gets all thin,
I guess I'll appreciate
your gentleness then.

And if I go first,
I know you'd hate that,
but would you take care of
my mom and my dad?

Khakis and cashmeres and
unsweetened tea.
You raising your eyebrows
flirting with me.

I'm sure it'll be fabulous—
totally fine.
Never thought I'd make it that far
but with you, I don't mind.

Higher Ground

It's a downhill walk from the castle to my flat
winter wind licked my skin, blowing straight through my slacks
between the top and the bottom of that slope, I reformed
I saved myself from salvation—the reborn was reborn:

God, can You hear me? I did my very best
My limbs are going numb with this guilt on my chest
O God of the universe! You know my fucking name
You count the hairs on my head. You gave me this frame.
You said, "Just come to me, child, and I'll do all the rest,"
and I came to You Son-bleached, my colors repressed.
What should I do now, Thou Most Holy Creator?
Deceive an innocent woman and come out as gay later?
I read all of your words and I prayed and I fasted
You neglected to heal me of this fatal attraction
I asked You over and over to make this queer straight
Your lack of action has sealed in this fate
You are the one who said, "Truth will set free,"
so this marks the end of me hating me

Love,

Calvin Arsenia

**Calvin Arsenia albums
available by Center Cut Records**

CenterCutRecords.com

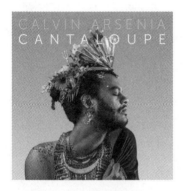

Comedian Justin Randall and musician Calvin Arsenia dive into their pasts as super Christian kids—we're talking wild times at church camp, speaking in tongues, and LOTS of sexual frustration—and explore how they've wrestled with their ideas of religion and deconversion in adulthood as queer entertainers. They also chat with other former Christian Kids and get the scoop on their journeys with Christ himself.

Have a similar story or questions to share? Call and leave a message at 913-283-4616 or email us at wewerechristiankids@gmail.com!

@imjustinrandall
@calvinarsenia
@christiankidpod

About the Author

Featured on *NPR, Pride,* and Grammy.com, Calvin Arsenia is a singer, harpist, composer, producer, author, and artist most known for *dazzling* the hearts, eyes, and minds of intimate audiences in oddly opulent settings around the world. After ten shame-ridden years as an Evangelical worship leader in the middle of America, Arsenia allowed performance and the art of song to rescue him from a fate of self-hatred to live a life spilling with wisdom, joy, and clarity.

Arsenia resides in Kansas City, Missouri, and enjoys cooking for his partner, watching foreign films, and planning his next big adventure. You can find more information about him at CalvinArsenia.com.

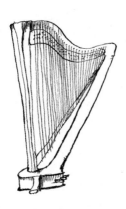

Enjoy *every good boy does fine* as an audiobook narrated by the author, wherever audiobooks are sold.

every good boy does fine copyright © 2021 by Calvin Arsenia.
All rights reserved. Printed in the United States of America.
No part of this book may be used or reproduced in any
manner whatsoever without written permission except
in the case of reprints in the context of reviews.

Andrews McMeel Publishing
a division of Andrews McMeel Universal
1130 Walnut Street, Kansas City, Missouri 64106

www.andrewsmcmeel.com

21 22 23 24 25 VEP 10 9 8 7 6 5 4 3 2 1

ISBN: 978-1-5248-6721-8

Library of Congress Control Number: 2021937313

Editor: Patty Rice
Art Director: Tiffany Meairs
Production Editor: Jasmine Lim
Production Manager: Carol Coe

ATTENTION: SCHOOLS AND BUSINESSES
Andrews McMeel books are available at quantity discounts with
bulk purchase for educational, business, or sales promotional use.
For information, please e-mail the Andrews McMeel Publishing
Special Sales Department: specialsales@amuniversal.com.